The Wealthy Child Workbook

Activities for Financial Education and Learning

Written by
Delvin Sullivan
with Kisha Freed

The Wealthy Child, Inc.
Huntsville, AL

Introduction

During my studies and travels while serving in the United States Army, I learned that 7 of 10 Americans have less than $1,000 in savings. Over 80% of the crimes committed that lead people to prison are related to money. With this knowledge, I decided to be proactive and develop a program that would introduce children to the world's economic process.

This program is called *The Wealthy Child*. The foundation of this program is built on seven pillars: generating income, budgeting, banking, establishing credit, making purchases (assets), investing, and giving back. If children learn the lessons in this book early on, we can greatly increase financial literacy and decrease prison sentencing amongst youth and adults.

This workbook complements *The Wealthy Child* book. Each section offers not only hands-on activities for practical learning with real-world examples, but also everyday financial math.

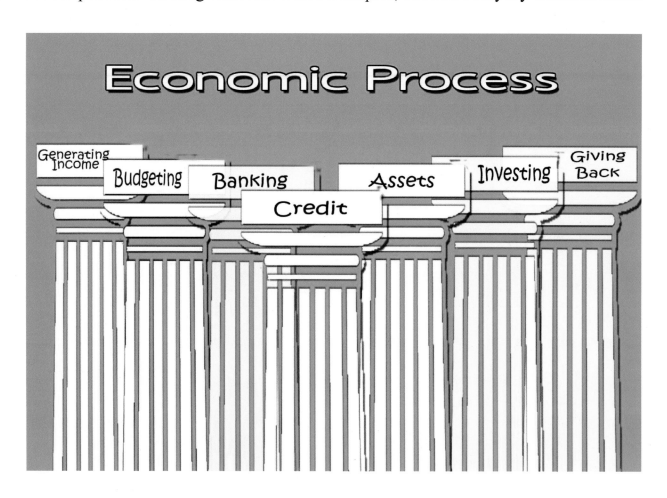

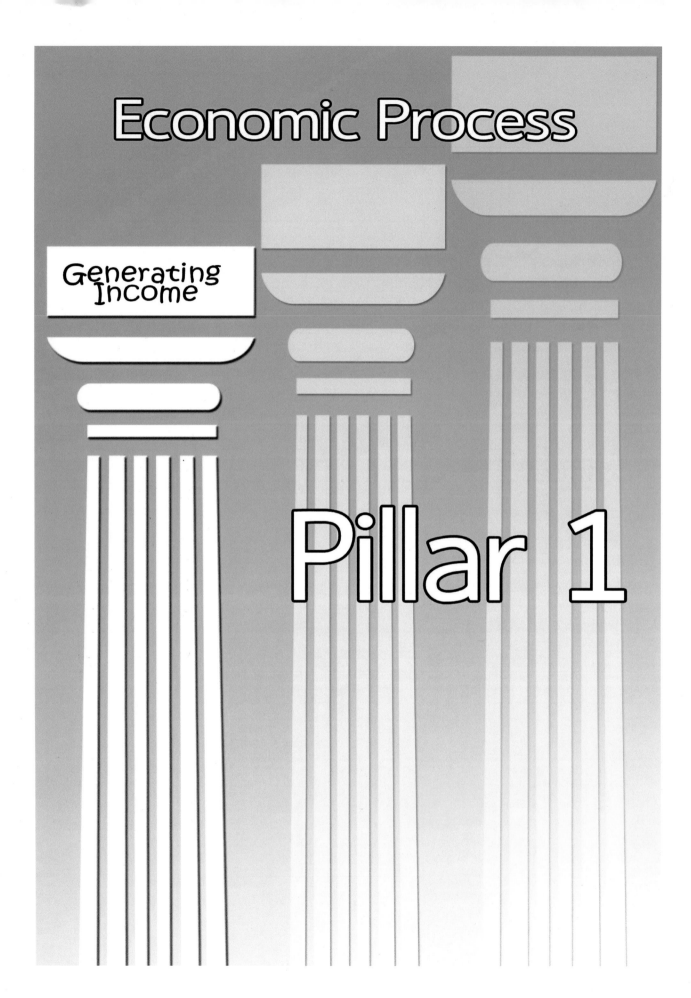

Economic Process

Generating Income

Pillar 1

Pillar 1 - Generating Income

In Pillar 1, Kamden wants a bike, but his mom says the family cannot afford to buy one. Kamden must now generate _money_ to buy a new bike.

1. What are two ways Kamden can generate income? *By getting a job and doing chores for people.*

Job Interview

2. When you go on a job interview, what three things should you remember to do?

- *Dress to impress*
- *Firm handshake*
- *Good eye contact.*

Operating a Successful Business

3. What are the 3 keys of operating a successful business?

- *Finance*
- *Marketing*
- *Operations*

Complete the definitions with the following words.

    finance   **operation**   **marketing**

4. The amount of money you need to run a business is called _finance_ .

5. A system of tasks that are performed to make a product or provide a service is an _operation_ .

6. The act of promoting a product to sell to your customers is called _marketing_ .

3

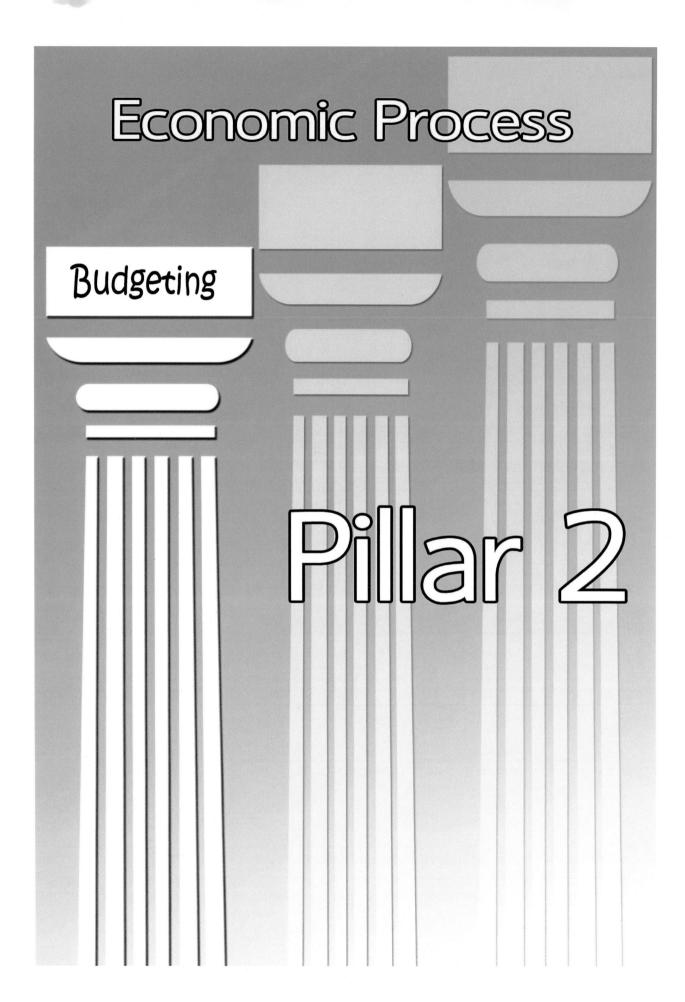

Economic Process

Budgeting

Pillar 2

Pillar 2 - Budgeting

In Pillar 2, Kamden gets his first pay check. He feels so happy! Unfortunately, this happiness does not last long, as he spends it all before he thinks about saving money for his bike.   Kamden realizes he need s to _budget_ his money and save so he can buy a new bike.

Draw a line to match the finance terms below with the definitions.

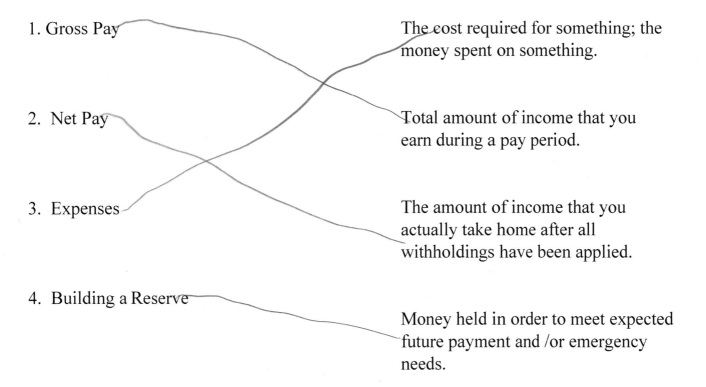

1. Gross Pay

The cost required for something; the money spent on something.

2. Net Pay

Total amount of income that you earn during a pay period.

3. Expenses

The amount of income that you actually take home after all withholdings have been applied.

4. Building a Reserve

Money held in order to meet expected future payment and /or emergency needs.

Gross Pay, Net Pay, and Deductions

To develop your budget, you must first take a look at how much money you earn. Review the sample pay stub below. Complete steps 1-3 at the bottom.

Advanced Heating and Air, 530 Crane Street Lake Elsinore CA 92530					EARNINGS STATEMENT		
EMPLOYEE NAME			SOCIAL SEC.ID	EMPLOYEE ID	CHECK No.	PAY PERIOD	PAY DATE
			XXX-XX-	062	370050	05/28/15-06/12/15	06/15/15
INCOME	RATE	HOURS	CURRENT TOTAL	DEDUCTIONS	CURRENT TOTAL		YEAR-TO-DATE
GROSS WAGES	28.00	80	2,240.00	FICA MED TAX	32.48		324.80
				FICA SS TAX	138.88		1,388.80
				FED TAX	360.78		3,607.81
				CA ST TAX	106.76		1,067.57
				SDI	20.16		201.60
YTD GROSS 22,400.00	YTD DEDCTIONS 6,590.59	YTD NET PAY 15,809.41		TOTAL *2,240.00*	DEDUCTIONS *659.06*		NET PAY *1,580.94*

Using the pay stub above, determine the GROSS PAY (blue box) and the DEDUCTIONS (yellow box) to determine the NET PAY (green box).

Step 1.   The current total is the **GROSS PAY**. Write the current total amount on the pay stub in the box labeled **TOTAL** (blue box).

Step 2.   Determine the total **DEDUCTIONS**. This includes federal taxes, state taxes, FICA Medicare, etc. Add each deduction amount and write the sum in the box labeled **DEDUCTIONS** (yellow box). This is the total **DEDUCTION**.

Step 3.   Subtract the **DEDUCTION** (yellow box) from the **GROSS PAY** (blue box). This amount is the **NET PAY** or your "total income". Write this amount as the **NET PAY** (green box).

Budget

After you determine your net pay, you can build a budget by mapping your expenses. Expenses, the money you spend, can include utility bills, groceries, and loan payments. Use the monthly budget below to create your own expense map and determine your total expenses, residual income, and reserve amount.

	Monthly Budget		
		Cory Jones	Student
1	Total Income	$ 4,000.00	3161.88
	Expenses		
2	Savings	$200.00	
3	Mortgage/Rent	$1,500.00	
4	Auto payment/Lease	$310.00	
5	Auto Insurance	$250.00	
6	Groceries	$220.00	
7	Credit Cards	$150.00	
8	Student Loans	$212.00	
9	Water	$40.00	
10	Electric	$195.00	
11	Cable/Internet	$67.00	
12	Phone/Cell Phone	$105.00	
13	Total Expenses	$3,249.00	
	Calculate Residual Income		
14	Total Income	$4,000.00	
15	Total Expenses	-$3,249.00	
16	Residual Income	$751.00	

To calculate your total income for your monthly budget, multiply your net pay on your bi-weekly paystub by 2.

For example, take the net pay you calculated on page 6 and multiply it by 2. This is the total income you will use on your budget sheet.

1. In the "student" column, fill in the **total income** (line 1) and **expense** amounts (lines 2-12) with your own numbers.

2. Calculate your **total expenses** by adding lines 2-12. Write the total amount on line 13.

3. Calculate your **residual income** by subtracting lines 14 and 15. Write the amount on line 16.

4. If you are paid bi-weekly, and you want to buy the latest video game console (PS4, XBox, etc.), how many pay checks (or how long) would it take for you to save the money to buy one? 4

5. ***Building a Reserve Fund:*** It is a good rule to build a six months reserve fund. To calculate your total reserve fund amount needed multiply your **total expenses** x 6. To determine how long it will take to save this amount, divide your reserve total by your residual income.

7

Economic Process

Banking

Pillar 3

Pillar 3 -Banking

In Pillar 3, Kamden puts his saved money in a sock. When he loses his sock, his friend Melissa suggests that he put his money in the_____.

Complete the sentences below by writing in the correct banking terms.

Checking account   **Money market account**   **Interest**

Saving account   **Certificates of deposit**

1. _____ is a bank account that earns interest as deposits are made and money retained.

2. _____ is a savings certificate with a fixed maturity date, specified fixed interest rate and can be issued in any denomination aside from minimum investment.

3. _____ is an interest-bearing account that typically pays a higher interest rate than a savings account.

4. _____ is a deposit account held at a financial institution that allows withdrawals and deposits.

5. _____ is money paid on a regular basis at a particular rate on money lent, or for delaying the repayment of a debt.

Answer the following questions.

1. What is the difference between a checking account and a savings account?

2. What is the difference between a savings account and a money marketing account?

Checks

You can write a check to withdraw money or pay an expense. Checks are provided by the bank and allow you to make financial transactions at any time or place with anyone.

1. Review the check below. The boxes marked with an (*) are the areas the check writer completes for purchases or transactions.

2. Now complete the blank check below with your name, date, and amount in the blanks.

Check number

Check Writer's Name

*Date check is written

Shirley Mitchell
817 Pine Park Drive
Huntsville, AL 35806

0011

*Payee's Name

January 3, 2018

Date

Pay to the
Order of   **Sam Johnson** $ 420.00

Four Hundred twenty and --00/100   Dollars

Capital Bank
www.bank.org 800-555-8899

For_____kitchen equipment_____   *Shirley Mitchell*

|: 254444689777|:   786547788002   0011

*Text Dollar Amount

Routing Number

Checking Account
Number

*Check Writer's Signature

*Numerical dollar amount

817 Pine Park Drive
Huntsville, AL 35806

0011

Date

Pay to the
Order of _____ $ _____

_____   Dollars

Capital Bank
www.bank.org 800-555-8899

For_____   _____

|: 254444689777|:   786547788002   0011

Understanding Your Bank Statement

Complete the sentences with the banking terms below.

withdrawal or debit   Deposit and credits

1. A _____ is an amount of money that is taken out of an account.

2. _____ are amounts of money placed into an account.

Every month you will receive a report from your bank which entails your debits, deposits and credits. This is called a **bank statement**. Review the bank statement and answer the questions below.

Bank Statement

If you have any questions about your statement, please call us at 816-234-2265	**Statement Date:**	**June 5, 2003**
	Page Number:	**1**

CONNECTIONS CHECKING Account # 000009752

Account Summary Account # 000009752

Beginning Balance on May 3, 2003	$7,126.11
Deposits & Other Credits	+3,615.08
ATM Withdrawals & Debits	-20.00
VISA Check Card Purchases & Debits	-0.00
Withdrawals & Other Debits	-0.00
Checks Paid	-200.00
Ending Balance on June 5, 2003	$10,521.19

Deposits & Other Credits Account # 000009752

Description		Date Credited	Amount
Deposit	Ref Nbr: 130012345	05-15	$3,615.08
Total Deposits & Other Credits			**$3,615.08**

ATM Withdrawals & Debits Account # 000009752

Description	Tran Date	Date Paid	Amount
ATM Withdrawal 1000 Walnut St M119 Kansas City MO 00005678	05-18	05-19	$20.00
Total ATM Withdrawals & Debits			**$20.00**

Answer the following questions based on the bank statement above.

1. What is the bank account number?

2. What is the beginning balance?
   On what date does the beginning balance start?

3. What is the amount of deposits and other credits?

4. What is the total amount of withdrawals / debits?

5. Were there any checks paid?   What was the amount?

6. What is the ending balance?
    What is the date of the ending balance?

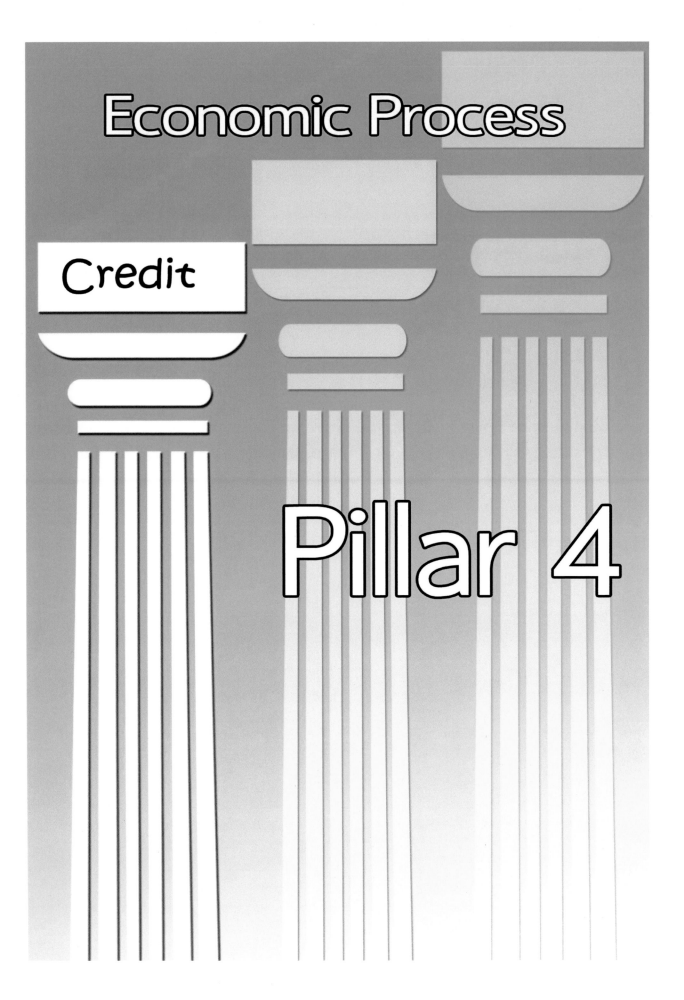

Economic Process

Credit

Pillar 4

Pillar 4 - Establishing Credit

In Pillar 4, Kamden wants to participate in a bicycle race that is taking place on the weekend, but he still has not saved enough money to buy a bike. Without having any established _____ , Kamden cannot borrow money to buy a bike. However, his friend Melissa is able to lend him the money so that he can participate in the race.

Match the following terms on the left with the definitions on the right.

1. FICO

Fair Isaac Corporation

2. FICO Score

The three main credit bureaus

3. Credit Bureaus

Companies that collect information relating to the credit ratings of individuals and makes it available to credit card companies and financial institutions.

4. Financial Institutions

A type of number created by the Fair Isaac Corporation.

5. Experian, Equifax, and TransUnion

Banks and credit unions.

Breaking Down Your Credit Score

(image not included here)

When you receive your credit report, you may wonder how your FICO score is determined. There are five main categories that are considered: (1) **payment history**, (2) **amounts owed**, (3) **length of credit history**, (4) **new credit**, and (5) **types of credit history**. Each category has an important impact on your credit score.

Categories of FICO Score

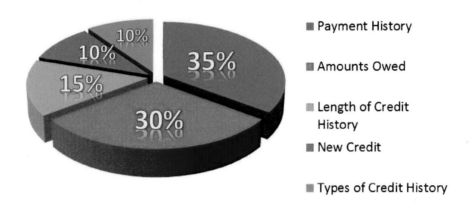

1. What percentage of your score is determined by **payment history**?

2. What percentage of your score is determined by **new credit**?

3. What percentage of your score is determined by **credit history**?

4. Which category has the **most** impact on your credit score?

5. Which two categories have the **least** impact on your credit score?

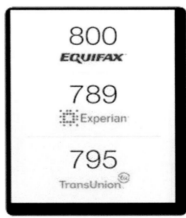

Sample FICO scores from the three credit bureaus.

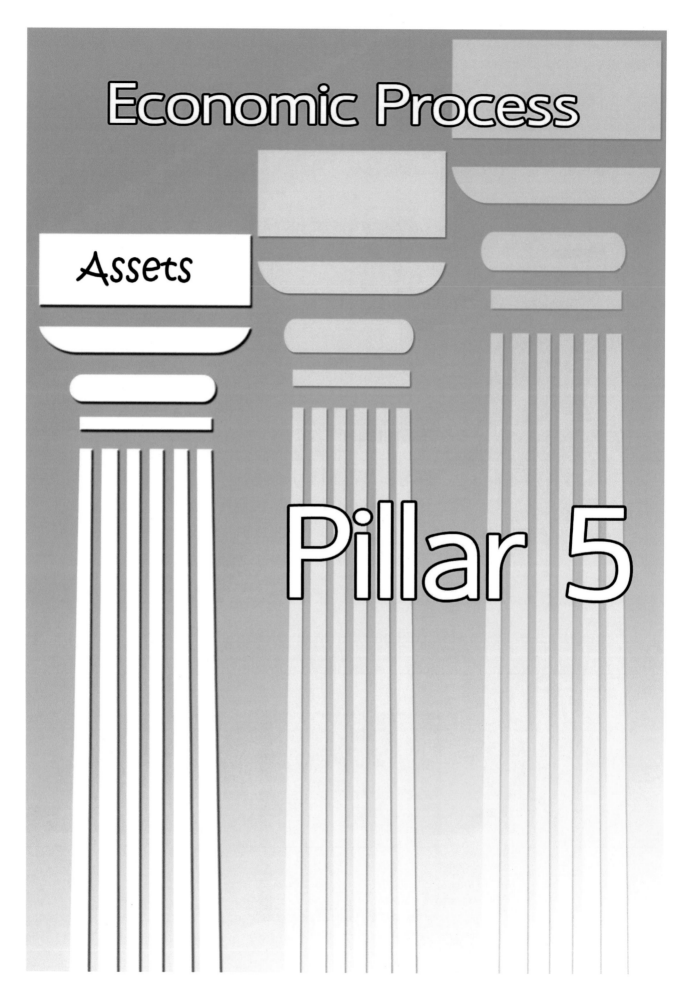

Economic Process

Assets

Pillar 5

Pillar 5 - Making a Major Purchase

In Pillar 5, after Kamden acquires his new bike and pays his loan to Melissa, he becomes interested in learning how to purchase a truck. Buying a truck is an example of making a major_____.

Complete the sentences with the terms below.

Debt-to-income Ratio   **Bank Loan**

Mortgage   **Negotiation**

1. _____ is all of your monthly debt payments divided by your gross monthly income.

2. A legal agreement by which a bank or other creditor lends money at interest in exchange for taking title of the debtor's property is a _____.

3. To deal or bargain with another or others property is called _____.

4. A _____ is the most common form of borrowing money for personal use or a business.

Major Purchases

1. Circle the examples of a major purchase or asset.

boat   refrigerator   piano   house   toothbrush

car   property   lamp

home stereo system   shoes   football

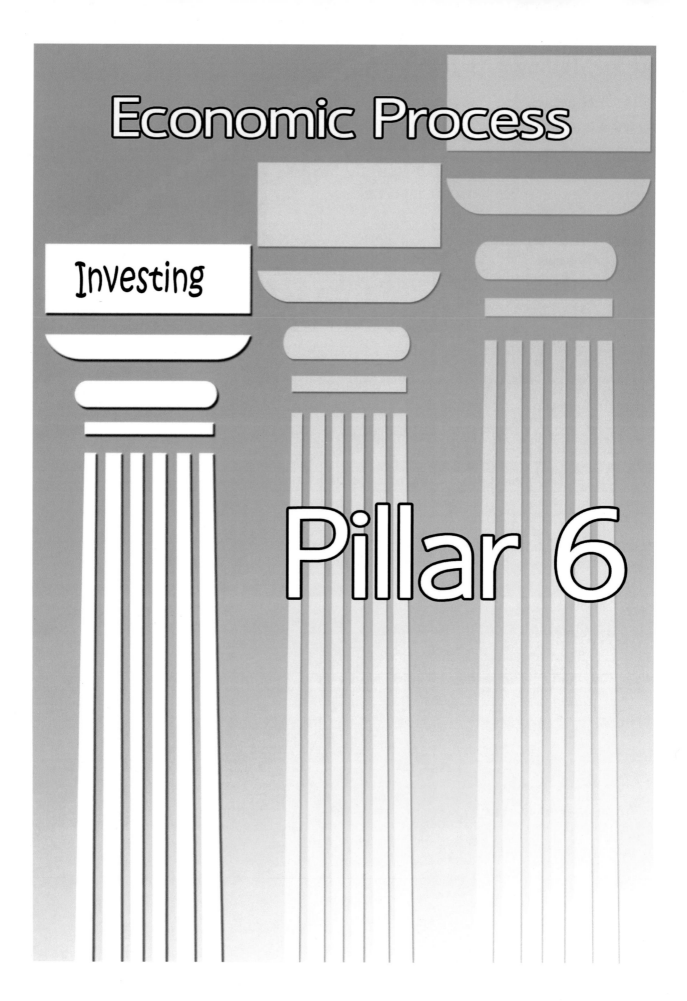

Economic Process

Investing

Pillar 6

Pillar 6 - Investing

In Pillar 6, Mr. Amir listens carefully to Kamden as he shares his research and knowledge about the Wheeled Lightning bike company. He then buys shares in the company so that he can make a profit. Mr. Amir is _____ in the Wheeled Lightning company.

Complete the following sentences with the terms below.

stock   **bond**

mutual fund   **Traditional Individual Retirement Plan (IRA)**

Roth Individual Retirement Plan (IRA)

bear market   **bull market**

1. A _____ is a debt investment in which an investor loans money to an entity (typically corporate or governmental), which borrows the funds for a defined period of time at a variable or fixed interest rate. Owners of bonds are debtholders, or creditors, of the issuer.

2. A _____ is a tax-deferred retirement savings account. You pay taxes on your money only when you make withdrawals in retirement. It comes in two varieties: deductible and non-deductible.

3. A _____ is a share in the ownership of a company. It represents a claim on the company's assets and earnings. As you acquire more, your ownership stake in the company becomes greater.

4. A _____ is a retirement savings account that allows your money to grow tax-free. You fund this account after you have paid taxes.

5. A _____ is an investment vehicle made up of a pool of funds collected from many investors to invest in securities such as stocks, bonds, money market instruments and similar assets.

6. A _____ is a financial market of a group of securities where prices are rising or expected to rise.

7. A _____ is a financial market of a group of securities where prices are falling and there is an expectation of an increase in stock sales.

Questions

1. What is the difference between stocks and mutual funds?

2. What is the difference between a Traditional IRA and a Roth IRA?

3. What is the difference between a bull and a bear market?

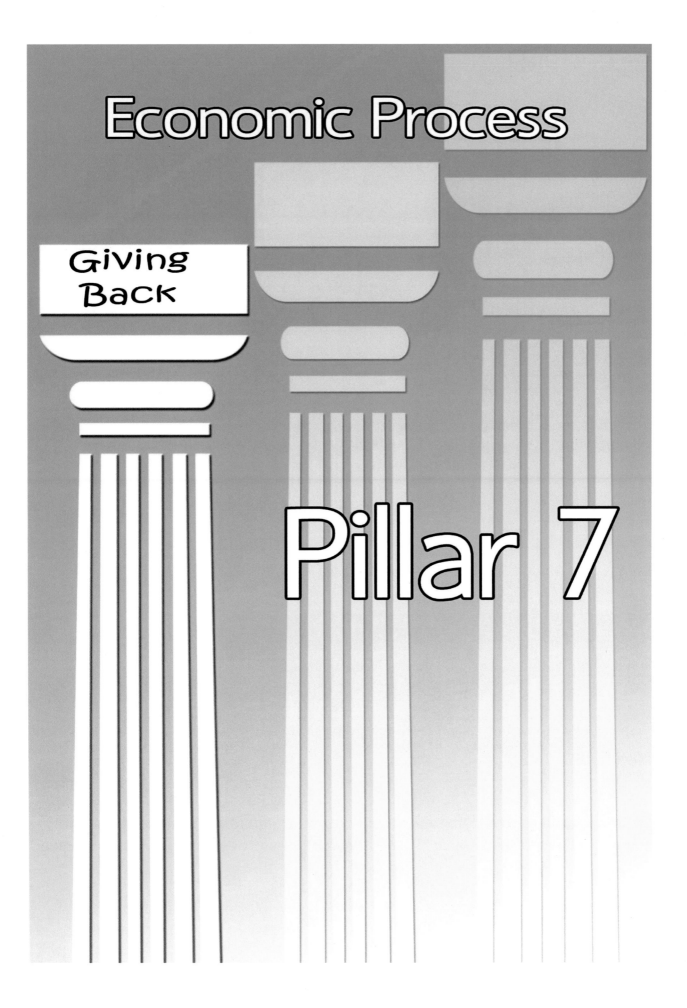

Economic Process

Giving Back

Pillar 7

Pillar 7 - Giving Back

In Pillar 7, Kamden, Melissa, and Mr. Amir plan a community service day for the World's Best Lemonade Company. Kamden realizes that his journey to becoming a wealthy child has been a gift, and so he chooses to _____ to the community by volunteering for the community service day.

Match the terms with the definitions.

1. philanthropy   unpaid work intended to help people in a particular area of need.

2. community service   a person who freely offers to take part in an enterprise or undertake a task.

3. volunteering   a person who has the desire to promote the welfare of others. This desire is expressed especially by a generous donation of money to a good cause.

Community Service

1. Research on the internet and find community service organizations in your area. What organization can you do community service for?

2. Write down a phone number for the community outreach coordinator for the organization.

3. Choose several dates and the amount of time you would like to volunteer. Call the community outreach coordinator to schedule one or more dates and times to volunteer.

About The Wealthy Child Non-Profit Organization

The Wealthy Child is a 501(c)(3) nonprofit organization established and designed to introduce children around the world to the world's economic process through the financial literacy workshop, The Wealthy Child.

In addition to offering The Wealthy Child workshop to churches, schools and colleges across the country and abroad, the organization also provides scholarships, prison and college tours, and educational supplies.

To schedule a workshop for your group, please contact Delvin Sullivan, founder of *The Wealthy Child, Inc.*, at (256) 468-3227.

For more information, visit our web-site: www.thewealthychild.net.

Math Calculations Sheet

Use this page to do the math for your financial wealth word problems!

Made in the USA
Columbia, SC
15 November 2018